Gallery Books
Editor Peter Fallon

THE WEDDING BREAKFAST

Frank McGuinness

THE WEDDING BREAKFAST

*Beloved darling Marianne
Love Always
Frank xxxx
Poem for Anita p. 40*

Gallery Books

The Wedding Breakfast
is first published
simultaneously in paperback
and in a clothbound edition
on 27 June 2019.

The Gallery Press
Loughcrew
Oldcastle
County Meath
Ireland

www.gallerypress.com

*All rights reserved. For permission
to reprint or broadcast these poems,
write to The Gallery Press.*

© Frank McGuinness 2019

ISBN 978 1 91133 769 0 *paperback*
      978 1 91133 770 6 *clothbound*

A CIP catalogue record for this book
is available from the British Library.

The Wedding Breakfast receives financial assistance
from the Arts Council.

Contents

Trains *page* 11
The Winter Coat 12
The Catholic Church in Garrison 13
Paul Léon 14
Orion 15
The Frogman 16
The January Turners 17
The Wedding Breakfast 18
Apples 20
Vietnam 21
The Jaw Box 23
Knights 25
Epithalamium 26
Burnfoot 28
Adieu 29
Cedar and Elm 30
A Haymaker's Jig 31
A Dream About My Father 32
Tullydish 33
Images at Ely 34
A White Horse 35
Easter in Venice 36
Chanson 37
Ogata Kōrin 38
The Bombay Scaffolders 39
Anita Pallenberg 40
Song for Carn Mountain 42
The Battle of Clontibret 43
The Bay Tree 44
Machu Picchu 45
Chicken 46
Yekaterinburg 47
The Grave 48
Odessa 50
Aeneas 51

The Crana River 53
The Mask 54
Morphine 55
Young Scientists of the Year 56
The Bus Ride to Fatima 57
Prudence Moore 59
Five Pound Note 61
Lucrezia Borgia 62
Heart Surgery 63
The Protestant Boys 64
Yukio Ninagawa, Director 65
The Folger Library 66
My Neighbour's House 67
My Father and the Mermaid 68
The Castrati Score a Penalty 69
Prayer to Apollo 70
Work Next Door 71
Spell 72
Syria 73
Kites 74
Who Could Survive the Atlantic Ocean? 75

1930s. Maginn Avenue, The Pound Lane, Buncrana, County Donegal. The women are my grandmother Lizzie O'Donnell and her neighbours, Liza O'Brien and Sarah Doherty. The little boy is Harry Ryan, and the gateway leads to my grandfather's forge over which I was born.

— F McG

Cover painting by Constance Markievicz, said to be a gift from the artist to Kathleen Clarke (widow of Tom Clarke, first signatory of the Irish Proclamation) while they were imprisoned in Holloway together. Kathleen Clarke, whose husband was executed for his part in the Easter Rising, was arrested in May 1918 and charged with involvement in the 'German Plot'. Maud Gonne was also in prison with them.

for Philip Tilling

Trains

That could be me, the red hair man
leading his child, his red-haired child
down the aisle of the moving train
travelling to Belfast — the child by the hand,
the boy looking at the back of his father,
holding each other by fingers and thumbs,
passing secrets on to each other,
secrets they'll tell to the end of days,
tucking each other into the clay,
reading stories passed from finger to thumb,
stories that begin, that end on a train
moving to Belfast, travelling from Dublin
where somebody says to himself,
that could be me, the red hair man
leading his child, his red-haired child.

The Winter Coat

Late September, it needs cleaning,
the winter coat, hanging in the hallway,
empty sleeves, empty pockets, boneless,
looking to be fed with wind and rain.

It never married husband nor wife,
kept itself to itself, the winter coat —
what yarns could it tell, stirring up bother,
taking both sides around the camp fire?

It has no fear of soldier nor priest,
though they might covet the winter coat.
Sabre and sacrament tore its lining —
we repaired it with haystack and needle.

Might it keep you safe in the dark,
the winter coat, warming your soul?
Sinner and saint, it's seen it all,
forgiving, forgetting, seasoned and soiled.

The Catholic Church in Garrison

for Orla Charlton and Stanley Townsend

Build a Catholic Church in Garrison.
Let its beauty take the eye from your head,
splendid as the secrets of Fermanagh,
witness to his touch, witness to my touch,
fingers feeling what was said, what was done,
all down the river now, best forgotten.
If you must weep, weep for Jerusalem,
the Stations of the Cross in Garrison —
a riddle of straight lines, a conundrum.
What kind of man would beg another stay?
He walks the streets of raw, enchanted towns,
chanting their names, their oceanic spell,
Belleek, Lisbellaw, Boa, Enniskillen.
Build the Catholic Church in Garrison.

Paul Léon

died 4th April 1942, Silesia

1

A horn of plenty summons Rhine maidens.
Two chairs, one table, maps of manuscripts.
A glass in the hand, a crack at its stem.
A drop of cognac might be just the job.

2

A man I know swallowed a dictionary —
tell me how tasty you found its blasphemy,
rich as the meat in a boeuf bourguignon,
red as fat wine on a cardinal's tongue.

3

I am the servant of some bits, some pieces,
treasures salvaged from papyrus orchards,
crammed into nineteen manilla envelopes,
the music of ghosts in deaf synagogues.

Orion

When my father muddled himself
with Orion the hunter
he chased fantastic prey
through strange Inishowen,
urging on his bread van
along the limb of the sun,
steering as if the stars
were earth beneath our feet.

These feet, these stars,
they were our guide.
I fill his shoes now
with the dust of our days,
seeing him ascend
leaving us behind,
implacable and cold.
He is hungry Orion.

The Frogman

for Johanna and Kevin

I saw him standing on Buncrana pier,
wrapped in algae and slippery as ice,
a frogman all the way from Atlantis —
was it Rathmullan across Lough Swilly?
His trunks turned blue from the cold of his breath.
Might he best be wearing a waterproof suit
dining to beat the band on meat and veg
the fecund sea produced for its children,
feeding them up as divine sacrifice
for the gods we worship? Why worship them?

That was the question I asked the frogman.
He declined to speak in simple English.
The effort to answer would have drained him.
Suffice to say he'd given nothing away.
Should he call himself a scuba diver?
Adamantly not — he was a frogman.
Kiss him, watch him turn into a chariot,
a coffin ship maybe, a banshee's wails,
a helicopter's broken frets and strings —
the frogman standing on Buncrana pier.

The January Turners

for Evelyn McDonald

They come from hibernation.
They smell of clean straw.
They dread cold water,
the fine wine of air.
They shake out their plumage.
Their pockets are deep.
They spend their pennies
on skies of ivory.
They down in one gulp
what's put before them.

They pay what's owed
with silver coins of their realm.
They control a kingdom
that's long been abandoned.
They build a house of straw
spinning while they sleep.
They dream of cold water,
the fine wine of air.
They live for daylight.
They love what kills them.

The Wedding Breakfast

We married last September in Belfast.
The Cardiac Unit, Royal Victoria.
Your heart surgeon said he'd do the honours.
I hear tell he was Greek, some Apollo.
He fancied himself another Dylan,
blood on the tracks like blood on the lancet.
Strumming your flesh with his swift fingers,
singing you safely home from the dying,
troubadour playing the pipes of your breath,
he phones to tell me it was near enough.

I did not dare ask, near enough to what?
We dread to think but must face the music
of what could have happened, so near, so far,
and here's me thinking, where should we both be?
Might we not have larks swimming on the moon,
some lunar crater where bees gather honey
sweetened by poisons spilling like mercury
drenched in the yellow blood of foxgloves,
an eye for an eye, a man for a man,
taking the plunge in a hospital ward?

Who made up the numbers of our wedding party?
What happy families — what foes or friends?
Who gave us gifts of cats' tails and egg shells?
Who played xylophones on my lover's shinbones?
What mad bastard suggested we do that?
Needles administer the wedding breakfast.
A champagne reception of Lucozade.
One groom wore the best of black pyjamas.
Our bridesmaid, the kind nurse from Hong Kong,
she who was wise as Jacob's Rebecca.

What did she make of our cracked *céilí mór*?
Who did she phone when she finished working?
Where was the sport, lads? What was the story?
Did she belong to a church of elders
demanding she shun all contact with queers?
Rewriting the Bible in Mandarin,
reciting Solomon's Song in Shanghai,
taking the piss out of Leviticus,
she brought us two rings, connecting claddaghs,
through Chinatown, Soho, weeping for Ireland.

Her boyfriend in Dublin had done the dirty,
a gazelle leaping over the Great Wall,
no chance of her walking down the aisle,
no more than ourselves till that lucky day
we went on a bender in Belfast City,
pledging our vows in that hospital ward,
risking the lives of our immortal souls,
the revels of fertile love between men,
enraptured in the Royal Victoria,
surviving heart surgery, sacred as gold.

Apples

for Briege and Willie Evesson

Cézanne
saw the cosmos
in a dish of
apples.

Bite,
and the universe
falls from a
tree.

Cézanne
heard the music
of spheres in
apples.

Taste,
and the galaxy
grows like a
tree.

Cézanne
read the tarot
in a plate of
apples.

Deal,
and the stars
are leaves on a
tree.

Vietnam

When I joined the trail, the Ho Chi Minh Trail,
heading southwards towards Dublin city,
it must have been the height of the bother
for we never ceased on our travelling,
never stopped for breath, never stopped for soup,
till we crossed the border, not looking back,
wrapping bombs in a cheese and ham sandwich,
letting kulaks pay for lunch, steak and chips,
in the Four Seasons outside Monaghan,
some way connected to Saigon city.

Imagine my glee when we fooled the forces,
the invading force from bluegrass Kentucky —
or was it Epsom Downs, the Knavesmire York?
We took them for a ride on hobby horses
wired to record all treasonable gossip
of stalwart whispers, plots to sabotage
attempts on the lives of Buddha, the Pope,
our mares themselves cut from finest bamboo,
piercing the feet of enemies enslaved
to socks, sandals, shoes — the best of leather.

We knew we'd take no prisoners, never,
teaching us the terror of blabbing yarns
should they smell dirty rats, combatants
in the army of our father, leading
us heading south towards dire Dublin
fighting for our liberation, free from —
from what, would someone kindly let me know?
What was the year? Nineteen seventy-one?
Were we entering Saigon or Dublin?

Who's best to tell me from those years ago?
Who now remembers tunnels beneath Slane?

Were the streets of Ardee hung with searchlights?
Did your heart break in two passing Omagh
knowing what was to come? What was to come?
The failure of the green revolution,
the dead dining on their young, on their dead,
devouring tulip bulbs, chrysanthemums,
sheer gold croci under an avalanche
that sweeps away the lost to Vietnam.

If the truth be told I know where to go —
I know where to find it, the lost country,
that red terrain, the bus from Donnybrook,
armies of volunteers stranded on board,
all on their own savage pilgrimage,
comrades together, the Ho Chi Minh Trail,
heading south to where? Towards Dublin.
Clutch at our chest miraculous medals,
repeating our vows of allegiance.
Loyal to whatever took your fancy.

I learned the hard way how to navigate
the Mekong Delta, its meanderings —
Mullingar, its choirs and its barber shops,
shaving beards behind knees, between the legs
of lads who cherished their former shipmates.
What became of them — the bald, the brainy?
Did they sing like nightingales spilling rice?
Scented rice, white, brown — something in between?
I hear tell few sleep soundly through the night,
dreaming of dead scholars, of Vietnam.

The Jaw Box

1

With our finest china I filled the jaw box.
Lending a hand, doing as I was bid,
the best laid plans and other come-all-yes,
how could I know scalding water cracked it?
Who'll stick together smithereens and shards,
the willow pattern's mystic sorrow?

2

I lean stupefied against the jaw box
hearing the news we'd won the war.
I'd witness once more the last of our name
stand where I stood, cleaning his hands, his bones,
soap twisting his eyes, face on a towel,
scraping from his soul vice and vanity.

3

Shirts he wore working doused in the jaw box.
They would never learn to hold their tongue,
pumping for news who made our daily bread —
baker's or butcher's delivery men.
My hands could read buttons, collars and cuffs.
Wonder they grew rough, learning such language.

4

Did we scrub infants in the same jaw box,
red-haired and roaring, hungry as lions?
We maintained water alone was holy
when for the first time the earth caressed us,
bathing in the warmth of far continents,
Africa asleep, dreaming of Asia.

5

Did you see their lips kissing the jaw box,
jammed to the brim with the best of china
broken like biscuits, shards and smithereens,
the willow pattern's mysterious sorrow?
Morning, noon and night what was the story?
Was it for the best no one breathed a sound?

Knights

after Bruegel the Elder, Frick Museum

I came across a hunter's bow,
a quiver without arrows,
illusions of fife and drum,
a shadow's mercenary.

I came across a torn shirt,
a gallowglass, a gamester,
illusions of fife and drum,
a bonnet without lacing.

I came across three birds in flight,
a pike and lances singing,
illusions of fife and drum,
the rising moon of morning.

Epithalamium

The husband fucked her
at the wedding breakfast.
She did not demur.
This marriage would last.
I'd say they are proud
of their place in the sun.
The children poured
from them like petroleum.
Might he bring to mind
her drunken father,
three sheets to the wind,
under the weather,
first thing in the morning
and last thing at night
beneath broken wings,
a sky without kites.

The husband fucked her
through the honeymoon.
She did not demur
though she thought him mean.
There's time when they sin
as he pokes and jags
she'd like to imagine
herself as a stag.
Her horns tear to shreds
his muscles and sinews,
staining the bed
where hyacinths grew.
So you might think
from the cries of the crowd,
fleshy and pink
as wounds from a sword.

The husband fucked her
as she gave birth.
She did not demur.
She knew his worth.
The child they conceived
grew into a man.
He felt like a leaf
in the palm of her hand.
A leaf that could wither,
a leaf in the rain,
a leaf called her father,
a leaf down the drain.
Her father came calling.
He knocked at the door.
Beneath broken wings
he fell to the floor.

The husband fucked her
at her father's grave.
She did not demur.
The marriage was saved.
I'd say they're still proud
of their place in the sun,
and children poured
from them like petroleum.
They run a tight ship
carved out of coffins
at each others' lips,
just as she imagined
whenever she burned
as he poked and jagged
and she was him turned
into herds of stags.

Burnfoot

Who would believe this? No way through Burnfoot.
The Derry road forks towards Buncrana —
for years it's been threatened, a fierce flood.
All hands tie in knots, this mad monsoon.

The River Jordan — make it our border.
Sacrifice of camels, sheep and oxen.
Will their screams defile waters of Burnfoot?

Sprinkle in torrents blood on the banshee,
her mark of Cain, his perfumes of Abel,
the kiss is the tell of husband and wife,
some story absolving Eve and Adam.

Build us a causeway — a bridge of pallets
fit for men to cross and fight with dragons,
raising from their graves the quick and the dead.

Adieu

Through our life I endured your rejection.
Too late now to change what always was done.
I who gave birth in your hall of mirrors
wonder what this marriage ever was for.
A man and woman entangled in touch —
when push comes to shove — don't amount to much.
Notes on the fridge chill the marrow and bone
that heard sweet nothings whispered on the phone.
Nothing is sweet after years of regret.
I put a curse on the day we first met.
May you know my wedding vows were lying.
May your sons mock you as you are dying.
Fetch me a hammer, some wood and some nails.
I'll build your coffin from my widow's wails.

Cedar and Elm

Ships smelling of wood, cedar and elm,
trim their sails by the trade winds —
they measure the map of Ireland
stitched on my mother's pincushion.

Living two doors down from the sun,
she worships at sacred mountains
in awe of ash and volcanoes
where forests grow cedar and elm.

A Haymaker's Jig

Clothes in the shape of somebody snoozing,
who left the bed like a haymaker's jig?

Trousers at half-mast, the lazy man's suit,
who's on parade like a haymaker's jig?

Baking scone bread with treacle and raisins,
who let it burn like a haymaker's jig?

Fairy lights drooping in all directions,
a Christmas tree or a haymaker's jig?

Chairs, tables break as you look at them —
carpenters dancing a haymaker's jig.

A Welsh dresser decked in melodeons,
music that's playing a haymaker's jig.

Holes in the cosmos — shoes black as your boot,
put it all down to the haymaker's jig.

A Dream About My Father

The Northern Lights, they erupted this year,
I dreamt about my father, him dying,
dying alone, crying out for neighbours,
as if the sun, the sky, my mother the moon
and every star above our heads ruling our hearts,
could contain themselves within his body,
no longer the frail thing of flesh and bone,
laid out, broken, on the kitchen lino,
terrified of blood, of bleeding to death —
and me not there, no one — none of us there
to hold his hand, no one to touch his face,
to whisper any words to comfort him,
to hear his voice echoing like a child,
calling father, father, father, father . . .

Tullydish

1

I wear armour forged in the mines of Tullydish
where the god, Hermes, abandoning the heavens,
took human shape — pirate and concubine
bleating like billy goats, looking for mercy,
sheltering from sin in the fields of Tullydish.

2

A sacred rumour — Hermes rules Tullydish,
mines yielding bronze worth a pretty penny,
pretty as sacrifice of sheep and billy goats,
blood sprinkles the townland, the shelter from sin
for pirates and concubines in Tullydish.

Images at Ely

The zodiac window, I'm sure, survives.
At Ely headless chickens rule the roost.
A zillion gods abandon the pews.
They have better things to occupy their time.

Pray for the damned at the zodiac window.
Cromwell plays with headless statues in hell.
That's where we'll celebrate the end of days:
a punctured star's celestial empire.

A White Horse

after Géricault

For years I dreamt a white horse
pretended to be seen
and took me against my will
to where I've always been.

For years I dreamt a white horse
answered to a name
and should I ever say it loud
my life would stay the same.

For years I dreamt a white horse
demanded the world know
when it rained — it always rained —
its fleece would turn to snow.

For years I dreamt a white horse
knew me well by name.
For years I dreamt a white horse
and myself were the same.

For years I dreamt a white horse
was all there was to know.
For years I dreamt a white horse
grew fleece as black as snow.

Easter in Venice

in memory of Constance Hayes Hadfield

The day they dragged me from my mother's paws
the doge committed original sin —
shoes on the table, the flowering haw.
Miracles happen each day in Venice.

Bricks in the bridge carouse the Rialto.
The lagoon waters turn our ships to stone.
Lie in the street, demolish fiascos.
A blast from your lips of 'Molly Malone'.

Venetians first, Christians second.
Who do we celebrate this Easter Day?
Emperor, sultan? The fat of the land?
Nothing is simple in Venice, we say.

Chanson

after François Villon

Where are the languid youths we once adored?
What curse has come about to maim them so?
Slender lads, they know the whys, the wherefores,
they played the game of smash and grab and go.
Thieves of our hearts, could they make grown men weep
and wash their faces with tears of shame and hate?
They fell with us into enchanted sleep
and woke to find their shadows grown fat.
Who now remembers when they shot the breeze,
so insistent on keeping their distance?
Who still worships — oh holy of holies —
at tabernacles tucked inside their pants?
Whose cock now do they prick tease but their own?
Who'll tell them beauty weathers into stone?

Ogata Kōrin

died 1716, Japan

I planted a garden of islands and plums.
A basket of petals bloodied the sea.
Feasting on ice, frost ate the garden.
Day turned to night in my fields of robe.

I had a fling with the god of thunder.
Our love turned every head in Kyoto.
The god of the wind ravished me with light.
Our fights were the talk of all Kyoto.

I planted a garden where wolves came to dine.
Big feeds of iris, carnation and moss.
The god of thunder, the god of the wind,
turned night to day in the fields of my robe.

The Bombay Scaffolders

1

Can they bear your weight,
those arms of skyscrapers,
seventy storeys ascending?
It's what you'd call a building boom,
every man for himself.
Polish your working boots.

2

Shelled like a lobster,
smelling of crab and mussel,
shaving their beards clean,
drinking pints of jasmine tea,
they are the last of their tribe,
time travellers in Bombay.

Anita Pallenberg

for Marianne

She dines in Knightsbridge, eating frugally.
The Roman waiters mock her gravitas.

They have no notion she speaks their dialect.
Italian plosives spit from her lips.

Silenced, chastised, they serve, heads bowed.
She sends back each dish to cruel kitchens.

I pay good money, I expect what's due.
Not filthy manners nor scratching fleas.

Peace offering, amoretti on a plate.
Unwrap a paper, set it on fire.

Falls to the table, singe of burning.
No lovely ascent to the cream ceiling.

What kind of joint cannot bake a biscuit?
These are fit only for discarding.

Come back to Tite Street, open a bottle.
Fix a time for a taxi to call.

Reserve warm welcome for those leaving.
Who knows whenever you'll see them again?

I once dined on snake with Queen Herodias.
They don't serve such fare in dainty Knightsbridge.

I asked for the head of John the Baptist.
It arrived shawled in leopard skin.

It must have dated from the end of the war —
Americans throwing gum they have chewed.

Each waiter tonight would have bared his ass
for the curving caress of the Yankee dollar.

Dreaming in French, in German, in Swedish,
I sang lullabies at the cradle of Europe.

What did I learn from the rubble of history?
Not to take shit in putrid restaurants.

Song for Carn Mountain

after Lorca

Why do you sleep alone, shepherd?
Why do you sleep alone?
In my bed you would sleep sound, shepherd,
why do you sleep alone?

Your sheet is spun from frost, shepherd,
your quilt is cut from stone.
Why do you sleep alone, shepherd?
Why do you sleep alone?

A woman's voice is crying, shepherd,
on this mountain of thorn.
In my bed you would sleep sound, shepherd,
why do you sleep alone?

Is there a child crying, shepherd,
on this mountain of thorn?
Why do you sleep alone, shepherd?
Why do you sleep alone?

The Battle of Clontibret

Fields in these parts of poppy or flax.
Winds blow whatever way they choose to fly.
Tough men in Monaghan burst into pink flame.
The wrath of God moves most mysteriously.

The angel of Clontibret will not let us forget
the jasmine of heather, the sour of success.
The same angel despoils bogs in the heavens,
driving uninsured, scattering the pikes.

The wrath of God moves most mysteriously.
His anger can inflame the flax and poppy.
Scowling and circling each magical square,
his angels once kissed their lord Lucifer.
He takes his bearings in lands time forgot.
His legions fight the Battle of Clontibret.

The Bay Tree

How long will it last,
the bay tree, you think?
Gardens change.
What was sturdy once survived.
These days, not so.

Just look at the moon.
The wax — the wane,
seasoning the soil,
ebb and flow of days.
Worlds shift.

Blame the moon for
turning nature unnatural,
just like myself:
blue as a bay tree,
green as the stars.

Machu Picchu

Some say it could be located in Kerry,
waiting to be found, lurking near Dunquin,
well defended, concealed by its Inca builders,
the strangest outpost of their breathless empire,
fluent in a Gaelic conquistadors had forgotten,
preferring to converse in some imperfect tense,
never the future, they have no use for futures,
stretching backward and forward as time pleased.

And nothing pleased the ear more in Machu Picchu
than hearing how master builders are worshipped
as messengers of the gods, the stealthy gods.
They measure sacrifice in hundredweights of blood,
shed for the pleasure of bodkin and fork, dirk and spoon.
Golden bowls catch the ash of poor folk's offerings —
a dozen duck eggs, pounds of butter, herring in creels,
such luxuries as delighted the same stealthy gods.

How should we depict them? Casual? Colossal?
Did they chew their long hair? Did they dye their nails?
Might the habit have given them the taste for flesh?
They say only those sharing divine lineage
were allowed don dark business suits, wristwatches,
blue shirts, ties the colour of clouds bringing rain
to irrigate the plains, allowing architects
to sustain the great citadels of Machu Picchu.

They fed on the fear of drought and famine.
They worshipped the chance of one in a million.
They ate the face of the goddess of fortune.
They stored chrism like seeds in their tall barns.
Remains of those barns were found on Skellig Michael,
buried with the children of lighthouse keepers.
They race up and down the scary stone stairway.
They whisper to us, Welcome to Machu Picchu.

Chicken

Sharing a flat
Anna Villas
Friday night food
legs wings and thighs
bony and golden
breaking skin
Kentucky Fried Chicken
smells of flesh
melting the suburb
silent Ranelagh

Saturday morning
Grafton Street
all to myself
the Eblana Bookshop
the Liffey bloodied
O'Connell Bridge
Kentucky Fried Chicken
legs wings and thighs
singe and bone
silent Ranelagh

Dublin, May 17th, 1974

Yekaterinburg

Our volleyball team, they're close to greatness.
No one can explain their feline prowess.
Their team colours mix motley with sickles.
At half-time they drink coconut water.
The deaf and dumb sigh at their agile limbs.
Some amongst them want an asteroid to hit.
The others pray to our heathen goddess.
They ask archangels to protect the earth.
Wrap us in feathers, Gabriel, Michael.
Show us the way to go home, Raphael.
Home to the holy city of Yekaterinburg,
blood on the walls, diamonds in the corsets,
red of the river, birds in mineshafts,
girls through a mirror, men up on a roof,
whispering secrets they already knew,
the serfs and soldiery in on the act.
Passing the time with games of volleyball,
admit to nothing in Yekaterinburg.

The Grave

1

I leave flowers on the grave, my father.
He who never did a day's work gardening,
who let the cherry blossom fall unnoticed,
who did not give a sinner's curse
where the same cherry blossom fell
from trees planted in the dream of our garden.
The garden sang songs each New Year's Eve.
The Scotch were there in assorted hoards.
The Scotch singing of Aberdeen and Dundee.
I met a Buddhist monk on the road there.
I gave him bits of chicken to eat.
Next thing we knew he was driving a car.
He howled in a nightmare of hotel rooms.
That's where you glimpse the Northern Lights of home.
The sun at midnight — the moon, when it liked
to do its disappearing act, the chance
that time itself is a matter of choice,
such crazed, curious, such games of give,
of take, when love is lost, when love is won,
when losing, when winning, when all that is
boils down to who's in the bed, when no one
ever is in bed with nobody, when
it no longer matters — what matters is loss.
Since love had done the business elsewhere,
love always does its business elsewhere —
where would be telling — so tell, tell, be done
with lies, let the truth free you. For what?
This is not time to pass. Say what you mean.
I leave flowers on the grave, my father.
I leave flowers on his grave, my father.

2

I leave flowers on the grave, my father.
He shakes himself awake, gardening.
His butterfly net caught cherry blossom.
He is a sinner, and I hear him curse
whoever fells the cherry blossom trees.
Who is it fells the cherry blossom trees?
Trees planted in the garden of his dream.
New Year's Eve, the garden went on the rampage,
crossing the border, letting loose its hoards —
the Scotch destroying cakes in Dundee,
the Scotch seeing the light in Aberdeen.
That's where I met the Buddha, Aberdeen.
He served me buttered bread and chicken.
He let me drive his car, though I chose not.
He howled in our nightmare of hotel rooms.
I did deny the northern kiss of home.
The sun at midnight danced, the moon did moan,
it did its disappearing act — it chanced
that time itself was a question of choice.
Such crazed, curious — such games of take
and give, when love is won, when love is lost,
when winning, when loving, when all that matters
boils down to who's denying whom, when none
deny they're not denying, when matter is loss
since love has done the business elsewhere —
where would be telling — so tell, tell, be done
with lies, let the truth free you. For what?
It is time, time to pass. Say what you mean.
I leave flowers on the grave, my father.
I leave flowers on his grave, my father.

Odessa

Russia lay siege to my dear.
He fasts for centuries,
declining trays of caviar,
spices from the Indies,
all that devils brandish.
He overturns tables,
harbouring his secret wish,
a price beyond roubles.
What would he buy, given gold?
Where would he spend silver?
A ship to hide within its hold
flowers that do not wither.

My dear could cross seven seas
as black as a Cossack's boot.
He built our house high in a tree,
a crown of thorns its root.
He gave me this ring to wear,
melted from samovars.
He shot the czar, as I desired,
he perished in the war then.
I kiss the icon where he lives,
a saint of gold and silver.
I place flowers on his grave,
flowers that do not wither.

Aeneas

1

When my father came
from his grave
in the story of Oedipus
to tell me
I would marry
my mad sister
should I not leave Carthage
I took this as sound warning,
he being expert
at incest,
Oedipus, that is,
not my father —
there and then I upped anchor.
The widow Dido
caressed our shadows
as if they were panthers
bred to do her bidding
ridding the house of rats
feeding on my hair,
delighting in its lice,
she siring a son,
creating daughters,
making me a promise
that I would believe
were she not past childbearing,
were I not at her beck,
were I not at her call.

2

When my father came
from his grave
in the story of Oedipus
to ask me
why was she cursed,
your mad sister,
should you stay in Carthage?
I took this
as sound warning,
me being expert
at departing
from burning cities,
from burning temples,
from burning fathers.
The widow Dido
caressed my backbone
as if we were sisters
bred to do the bidding
of our dying father,
worshipping the panthers
licking our hair,
cleansing it of lice.
They filled us with sons,
identical daughters,
each making a promise
we would both believe
were we not burning
in our father's temple.

The Crana River

They waded across the River Crana,
our grandfathers, uncles, grandmothers, aunts,
hiding inside trees gold, frankincense, myrrh,
bringing rain that does not know when to stop,
rain that teems drenching only this parish,
Urris, Lisfannon, Swilly Terrace, Cockhill,
taking it in turns to disembowel
walls, doors, weeping curtains, soaked with soft wind
flattening the goalposts of playing fields,
abandoning Gaelic, soccer, hurling,
raising the water beneath the Mill Bridge,
a bridge built to last all eternity,
the world gone crazy wherever you stand,
fearful of lightning, torrents of thunder,
the place we call home, home turning to rain
bringing rain that does not know when to stop,
rain that says something nobody else says,
rain crashing to earth in vowels and verbs,
a reason of rainbows, the Crana River.

August 21st, 2017

The Mask

Become a god in whom I can believe.
Take stock of my strange, devout prayers.
Work a miracle to my advantage.
Fill me with golden dust — I am empty.
Trace in that dust an image carved from stone.
Let me graze in a field of tesserae.
I am the meat and the drink of heaven.
You hear me ask why you nuzzle a knife.
Has it been fashioned to your instruction?
Make something splendid to kill my brother —
something blinding and pure, like the sun.
Catching your tears in a goblet of glass
he would not hesitate to smash the snow
back into the substance of sea and sand.
Beat it senseless then into what you crave:
a mask in the shape of a fox and hare,
the two breeds ripping their lining apart,
drinking the blood of prodigal sons
who knew better than to venerate gods.
No — they much preferred handmaidens
schooled in the alchemy of elegance,
raising the spectre of dragons in heat
brandishing fabulous, ivory tails,
feeding as you'd fatten a golden calf,
seeing the world through the eyes of its mask.

Morphine

The first time taking morphine,
an earache splitting my brain,
pain turned into howls of laughter.
One minute, agony — the next,
in convulsions — cackling, a joke.

Is that boy mocking us or what?
Aunt Eileen asked my mother.
All I know was we could fly
to the sun in the ceiling.
Orbs of electric light.

Sleep came then easy as love
giving wings in my parents' bed.
The sky touched our roof tiles.
All hands free from sorrow,
the first time taking morphine.

Young Scientists of the Year

How we hated them, snug in uniforms,
wanting to tear ties knotted at the throat,
whisper depraved, unfathomable charms
in their waxless ears, leave them black as soot.

Cut their wires, pull the plug from computers.
Wet them with holy, poisonous oil —
hypotenuse, triangle, odd numbers,
turn them rich and strange as water that boils.

Body is mind's architecture of bone,
ghosts that perspire in the ether of steam.
Free the mathematics of magical zones.
Square the circle where two lovers dream.

The Bus Ride to Fatima

1

Might we look at the markings on marble,
a red slab of soap, a map of India,
Henry the Navigator wiping his hands?
Exploring the lower deck of his ship
he stumbled upon a cargo of unicorns,
one of whom called herself his own mother.
Handing him a bullet she begged to be shot.

Did this happen at the shrine at Fatima?
How did we get there? By bus ride of course.
The passengers were all in need of a cure —
remedy what? The world and its sorrows?
Prince Henry sailed to his city of streets.
He'd down pints in one and stagger back home.
Refrain from passing champagne to that bozo.
Drunk, he might very well miss the miracle.

2

What then will become of us, sensing the worst?
Why hope for the best, fearing all we know?
The Prince has deep pockets, he pays out escudos,
spare coinage of strange denomination,
minted to serve the Emperor's fierce whims,
a Mikado of Spain, Caesar of Portugal.
He joins us on the bus ride to Fatima.

He nurses incurables, he heals the sick.
They stand, they slobber, dance on their death beds.
Hotels are rabid with fervour and mercy,
with the glee of the Virgin giving birth —

birth to bleeding feet, Brazil and its children
as they cross continents, displaying
restraint, proportion and harmony,
defying tyrants on the bus ride to Fatima.

Prudence Moore

Wandering, wandering,
Prudence Moore, I see behind me.
There she goes, watch her —
she meanders the shore front.

Smelling of honeycomb,
her sister, Eileen Moore,
graced the tennis courts,
the putting green.

Patience lost direction
on St Columba's Avenue.
She is not well at all,
the town whispers.

Gasping her last breath
poor Eileen goes first,
forgetting every rule,
regulation and reform.

The Moore family's fortune —
what of it remains?
A few ruined acres
near Ards monastery.

Who keeps the wolves
from their scullery door?
Monks, monks, monks,
nothing but monks.

If Prudence is simple
then so too is fortune —
wheels that rotate,
somersault and spin.

Look, there's my father
leaving Paddy Barney's shop,
seeing Prudence cross the road,
leaving her safe.

Look, there's my father,
beneath Eileen's coffin,
carrying her corpse —
is she not a neighbour?

Yes, the very best.
Did us many a good turn.
Should she not be given
the last lift?

Five Pound Note

Thin as snow and smelling of papyrus,
a five pound note that came from Alaska,
all robed in purple like an emperor.

My father's neighbour, just home from the States,
pressed it into my Communion paw,
a wage to appease gods of Donegal.

I had then received the sleep of reason,
expansive tundra, numb as Alaska,
treasure buried in my mother's blue purse.

When did we spend it? Not that long after.
Why did we need to? For winter fuel.
Where is it now — the snow of papyrus?

Lucrezia Borgia

I broke a mirror across my lover's head.
Who was it poured milk in his mercury?

He dressed me in leaves of mulberry trees.
He placed on my face a mask cut from lead.

Heart Surgery

My love, he's an Olympic champion.
Wimbledon? He's won more than seven times.
As a boy he survived pogroms in Kiev.
As a girl she called Joe Stalin father.
Where on earth can we find the motherland?

How about Coleraine, among green, green bushes?
The roundabout, beside the Lodge Hotel,
cars spinning, heading for Portrush, Portstewart,
in each a new heart beats for my lover,
lying buried deep in dunes and soft sand.

Dunes and soft sand, where he bared his body,
scarred, the knife's meticulous manoeuvre,
his bed the size of the Atlantic Ocean —
through polished windows he can see Scotland.
When he's well we'll walk there over the waves.

Old women's stories — who now believes them?
Old women in this ward, loved by old men,
holding hands as if love depended on touch,
touch and go, the give, the take of breathing,
years surviving pogroms, buried in dunes.

The Protestant Boys

The ship, *Euripides*, carried us south
far from the clamour of cursing mouths
naming and shaming us fatherless sons,
the pointing finger giving direction.

As the roots of fig trees let themselves go
in Connemara I can spell kangaroo.
Forty days, forty nights, our span of hire,
the world of distraction freed us from fire.

We betake ourselves from fields near Clifden,
as if towards Mecca, next year Jerusalem.
We cry no surrender, all hands in cahoots,
thin as a shoelace in Protestant boots.

Starved to survive, without mother's milk,
a salvation army, our uniform silk,
we greeted the new world, tamed, unsound,
on the ship *Euripides*, Australia bound.

The boys' orphanage at Ballymacree, Co Galway, was burned down by anti-Treaty Republican forces in July 1922 for allegedly teaching the boys to be pro-British. The majority were sent to Australia on the ship Euripides.
— The Irish Times, *20 February 2012.*

Yukio Ninagawa, Director

He measures the rainfall on Mount Fuji.
He reckons it safe to construct temples
carved from flotsam, jetsam, debris of days,
doing it again, again and again,
rehearsing, replanting the tree of life
shedding its blossom, its leaf from the branch,
staining the earth like ice on Mount Fuji,
turning aside the eyes of all the gods,
Shinto gods weeping for one of their own,
flotsam and jetsam of heaven and earth,
resplendent, a most honoured gentleman,
constructing temples, leaf, branch and blossom,
doing it again, again and again;
practice makes perfect the music of spheres.

The Folger Library

Guess who I saw pass, as a ghost, through the Folger Library?
Whose was that shade carved a name on the admissions' desk?
Who denied he'd written a line of any book on display?
Who said if fire consumes this house then so be it?

There's no such thing as a ghost that haunts the Folger Library.
Slap a writ on that shade, do not grant him admission.
Why deny writing a line of a book carved from air,
from water, from earth? If fire consumes him so be it.

How did the funds stretch that supplied the Folger Library?
We traded in ghosts, dabbled in shades, charged for admission.
Hoarding silver nickels and dimes we bought golden inkwells
dripping like fountains, swallowing nibs, penning so be it.

Guess who I saw burning to death in the Folger Library?
Bring me the shade manning the desk, refusing admission.
Guess his answer when quizzed, what have you ever written?
Why clap his hands and disappear, whispering so be it?

My Neighbour's House

in memory of Mick Muldoon

Spread honey on my neighbour's house
where bees make good companions
coming from sweet Athy or Canada.
Time to start harvesting.

Pour wine on my neighbour's house
where one and one make three —
a ruby red arithmetic.
A great lake rotating.

Perched on my neighbour's shoulder
the moon lights up a match,
struck from a book of bone —
a shrine of ivory.

My Father and the Mermaid

for Bríd and Gerard Fanning

He knew where she lived before she was taken —
or drowned, as heretics chose to whisper.
Some say she changed into a parakeet,
a bird or flash of murderous petrol,
charring its wings, its feathers of rainbow
stretching from Alba to the Cliffs of Moher.
It's claimed she snatched her scalding of a child
from water stained green by her thieving hand.

The centaur lamented the loss of his son.
He should have known better than marry a mermaid.
How was she caught? Nails and pincushions,
stitching the leaves of Atlantic fields.

A friend to all men, a shell to no snail,
four feet and a tail, mermaid and centaur.

The Castrati Score a Penalty

They came since they were wanted nowhere else.
Who put a name to a face amongst them?
Their fame had long vanished — hearts no longer stopped,
hearing their voices soar high as Mount Ararat.
With no whiff of scandal were they priests at all?
They'd come to bless our rites, our rituals —
baptism, penance and holy orders,
extreme unction, hands feeling the Eucharist,
men who had never disturbed the peace,
the peace that would pass all understanding
why an army of castrati invaded
every Gaelic pitch of our county,
slashing their wrists when the team played like dogs,
entangled in nets, celestial boots,
effing and blinding with strict harmony,
shocking the sisters who fed and clothed them.
When the castrati scored a penalty
it was a sign mankind was forgiven.
The ball disappeared into cobalt blue skies.
We shouldered them home — one died in our arms.
The press played a blinder, dishing the dirt.
What if these lads took a hand at us all
fooling their dogmatic congregations,
simple folk, easy-going men and women,
petrified touching the flesh of castrati,
removing their bits for love of a game
they played without blemish, without frenzy,
believing in God and in penalties,
the music of spheres, the incanting crowds,
singing goodnight, Irene, Irene, goodnight
at a screech the hounds of heaven could hear,
sent by their master to do their damnedest?

Prayer to Apollo

I built an empire
of Atlantic straw.
The ocean told me,
time to pick, to choose
what is your fate —
the juniper or haw?
Whatever your poison,
do you win or lose?

I constructed souls
out of stubborn bones
champing at the bit,
fit to be tied,
wearied unto death
by good-looking men
who swear by Apollo
never to wed.

Apollo forgives sins,
all his priests said,
ripping wings from us
like roasted birds.
Do they give a curse
where he lays his head?
Does he give a curse
whose prayer is heard?

Work Next Door

The work next door will never finish —
so my good neighbours must feel.
I would not enter their house unasked.
That's why I can see so little change.
They ask, do they disturb you, the workmen?
The noise they make, too much at times?
They stop, they start at the agreed hours?
Tell us if not, we'll pass on the word.

I place a glass upon this table.
I summon spirits to my aid.
The glass will shatter, or it will name
their builders laying siege to Troy
and fashioning for my good neighbours
a wooden horse — a home from home.

Spell

Stand to attention
spell out letters
round the room
around the room
thart ar an seomra

A sick boy turns Siamese
or is he from China
watch his face yellow
ask for the toilet key
an eochair le do thoil

A cage in the jungle
a bamboo cane
his palms purple
around the room
thart ar an seomra

Syria

1

I've started to suffer in confined places.
It's not that I back away from panic.
More I cannot bear mouths speak in faces
relaying evidence that could never stick.
Yet they insist I should bear all the guilt.
My regime uprooted thousands, millions.
Abandoning treasures winnowed in mills
where the chaff, the wheat are one and the same —
we deal in the foul business of disposing,
as if that were some great act of folly,
roughly on par with killing the king,
damning for eternity your mortal soul,
not that it matters if hell or heaven
readies itself to greet you as brethren.

2

What suffocates me in confined places?
All I recall is a sense of panic.
I hear accusations from mouthless faces,
tongues hitting harshly as balls on a stick,
played by children — no notion of guilt
to disturb the dreams of thousands, millions,
woven from linen in abandoned mills,
the fed, the wanting, the one and the same
well-versed in the foul art of disposing
whoever conjured great acts of folly,
never forgiven, like killing a king,
jigging a reel with your immortal souls,
bracing yourself with great fires of heaven
at the gates of hell, greeted as brethren.

Kites

After forty years
embracing tonight
I reach and touch
air between us.

Your body flees,
free as a kite,
a vein of flesh,
string tied to dust.

Who Could Survive the Atlantic Ocean?

i gcuimhne ar Danny Sheehy

Who could survive the Atlantic Ocean?
That's a fit question for a man to ask.
Some say the water's occasion of sin
allows us to don the penitent's mask,
confessing to waves right, left and centre
secrets concerning how life's to be led,
snatching forty winks stretched out on a chair,
or choose something else, a dream that dreams fed.

I long gave up guessing profit and loss.
Hand in trousers pocket, shell to your ear,
siding instead with the ships tempest-tossed,
their crews quite splendid in beautiful fear.
Where would they sink deepest, lough or lagoon?
Worshipping strange mutineers of the sun,
able to perceive the light of the moon,
believe this to the end — what's done is done.

So, it is over? *Consumatum est*?
Men at a party sing Dean Martin songs.
The moon hits the sky — a warren or nest?
A big piece of pie — the righting of wrongs.
Who stands offended in the red corner?
Gaelic speakers in the pine tree's shadow
send money home to starving mourners,
pounds, shillings and pence from *fadó, fadó*.

I know a fellow the sea created.
When I say created what do I mean?
I wish I could ask where it is he'd fled —
where is it he was? Where is it he's been?
Somewhere off the coast of Portugal,

the Atlantic ice, men in the water,
could I draw about you a Galway shawl,
I would be your wife, mother and daughter.

No point — you have embraced frostbite and cold.
No point — you have faltered, gasping your last.
As well catch the moon in its net of gold.
As well catch the sun in its hood of glass.
I ask from you only you take your time.
Smash the world record sailing round the globe.
Strike the oars like a bell that cries and chimes.
Let your body be dressed in mourning robes.

Are the robes the colour of black or blue?
Who can tell the difference between them?
The ones who endured what music can do.
Tearing the leaf from the blossom and stem,
arias of grief, girls, boys, forgotten,
lost in the sea's eternal song contest,
aping melodies of sparrow and wren,
they pretend to dine on Chinese birds' nests.

What was it then we hungry hoards devoured?
Cigarette packets, red lemonade bottles,
feeds of fragrant pork, flavoured sweet and sour —
there is no refuge between heaven and hell.
I listened to the humpback whales singing,
translated their sorrow into our speech.
Bad luck fell on all hands, the captains and kings.
I bear witness to what's beyond my reach.

Like the sand, the shore, when I carved on wood:
'Home is the sailor — abandon the sea.'
I refused to do that, by all I hold good

in rough and tumble, the heart's crazed decrees.
Each man for himself? No, never say die.
Above all be able to play down panic.
Times when it's better to just let things lie.
Ponder on heather, the hay in its ricks.